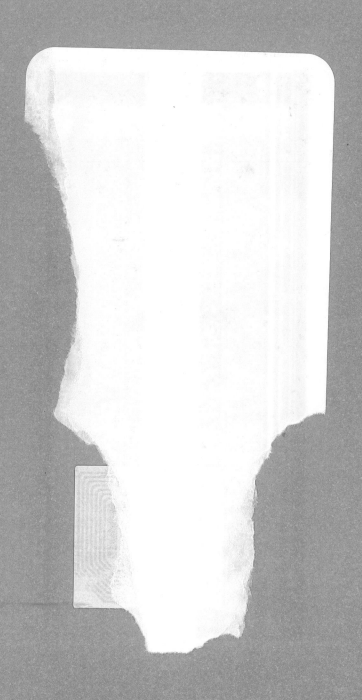

To Lee

E (JABC)

322-1887

SIMON & SCHUSTER BOOKS FOR YOUNG READERS
An imprint of Simon & Schuster Children's Publishing Division
1230 Avenue of the Americas, New York, New York 10020
Copyright © 2004 by Lisa Campbell Ernst
All rights reserved, including the right of reproduction in whole or in part in any form.
SIMON & SCHUSTER BOOKS FOR YOUNG READERS is a trademark of Simon & Schuster, Inc.
Book design by Greg Stadnyk
The text for this book is hand-lettered by the author.
The illustrations for this book are rendered in cut paper.
Manufactured in China
10 9 8 7 6 5 4 3
Library of Congress Cataloging-in-Publication Data
The turn-around, upside-down alphabet book / Lisa Campbell Ernst.—1st ed.
p. cm.
Summary: An alphabet book in which each letter becomes three different objects as the
book is turned different directions, as when A becomes a bird's beak, a drippy ice-cream
cone, and the point of a star.
ISBN 0-689-85685-7
1. English language—Alphabet—Juvenile literature. 2. Toy and movable books—Specimens.
[1. Alphabet. 2. Toy and movable books.] I. Title.
PE1155 .E76 2004
428.1'3—dc22   2003016318

The Turn-Around, Upside-Down Alphabet Book

LISA CAMPBELL ERNST

Simon & Schuster Books for Young Readers

New York London Toronto Sydney

A becomes

half a butterfly,

two windows in a castle tower.

B masquerades as

C pretends to be

a teacup handle,

D turns into

candles on a birthday cake.

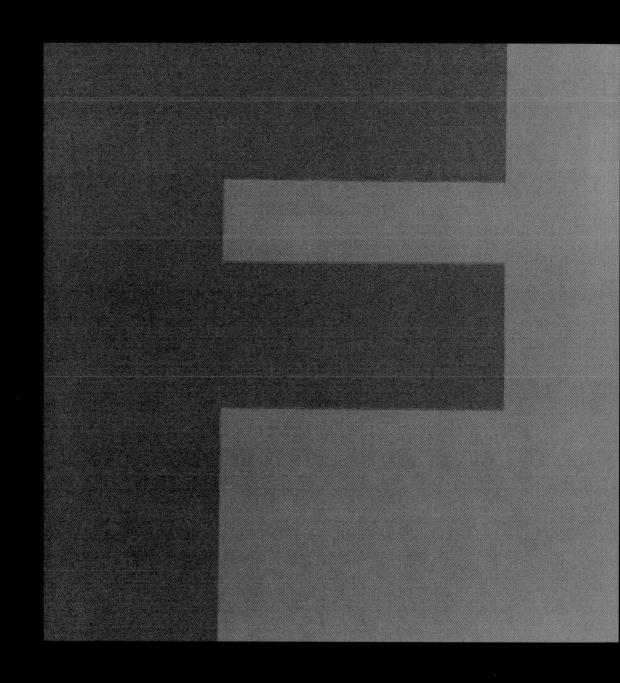

a lobster claw,

a reindeer's antler.

F imagines itself

a scooter's back wheel,

a magic wand casting a spell,

a fishing hook.

G becomes

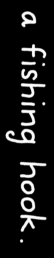

H masquerades as a train track,

waffle squares.

a waterfall,

a birthday present with a blue ribbon.

I pretends to be

a candy cane,

an elephant's trunk,

a monkey's tail.

J turns into

K dreams of being

a cell phone,

L imagines itself

the top of a cathedral,

two fish playing chase,

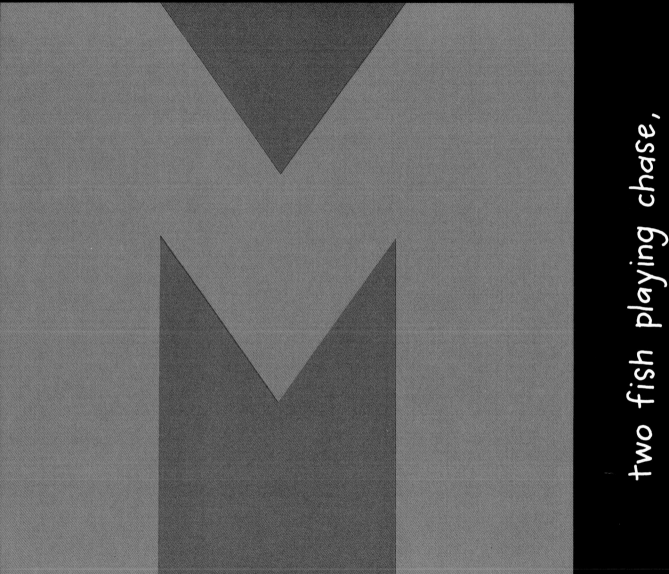

M becomes

a gopher's tunnel,

two tortilla chips headed for guacamole.

N masquerades as

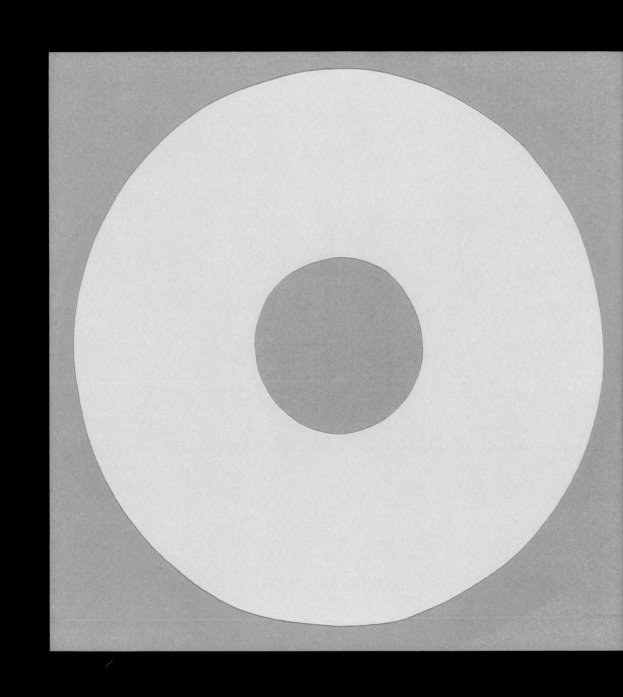

an owl's eye,

a fried egg.

O pretends to be

a gumdrop being tossed into an open mouth

a seed being dropped into a hole,

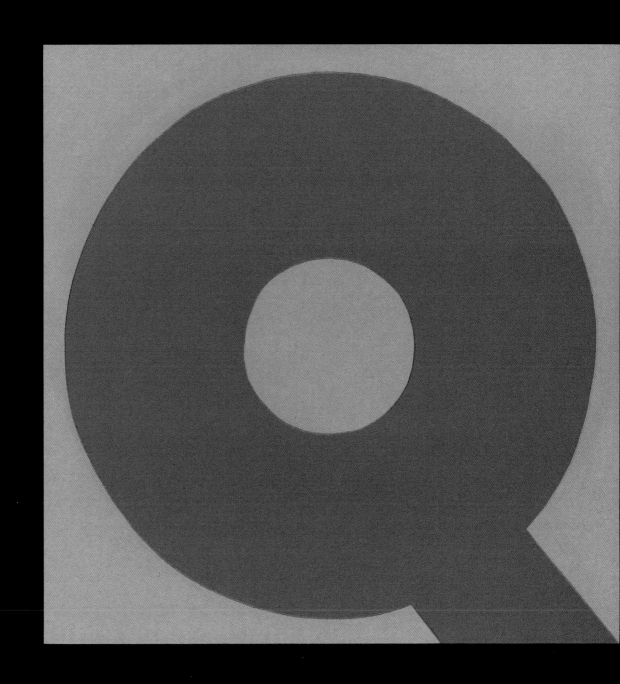

a pendulum on a clock,

a tag on a dog's collar.

Q dreams of being

a rabbit,

R imagines itself

S becomes

a clown's top hat,

Pinocchio's nose.

T masquerades as

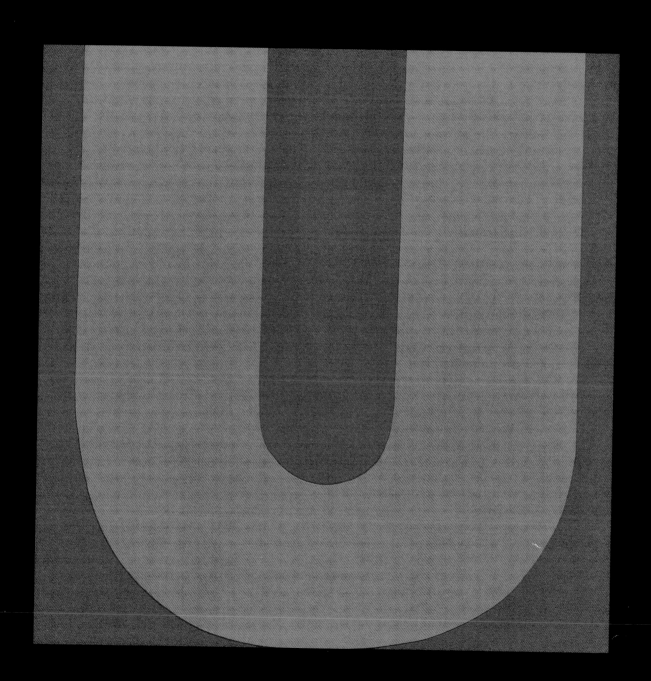

a droopy mustache,

a hot dog on a bun.

a magnet,

U pretends to be

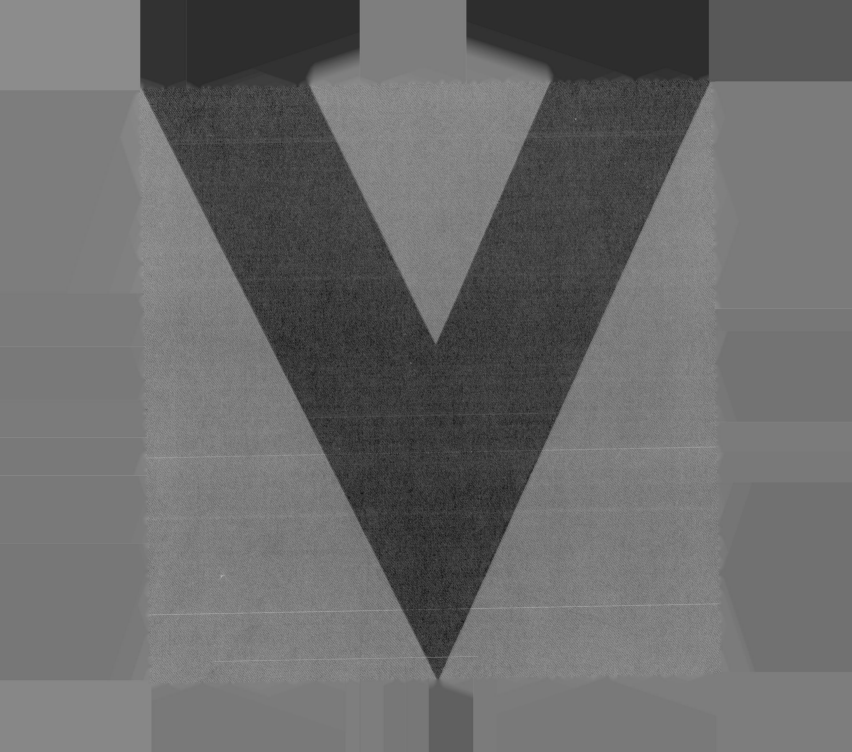

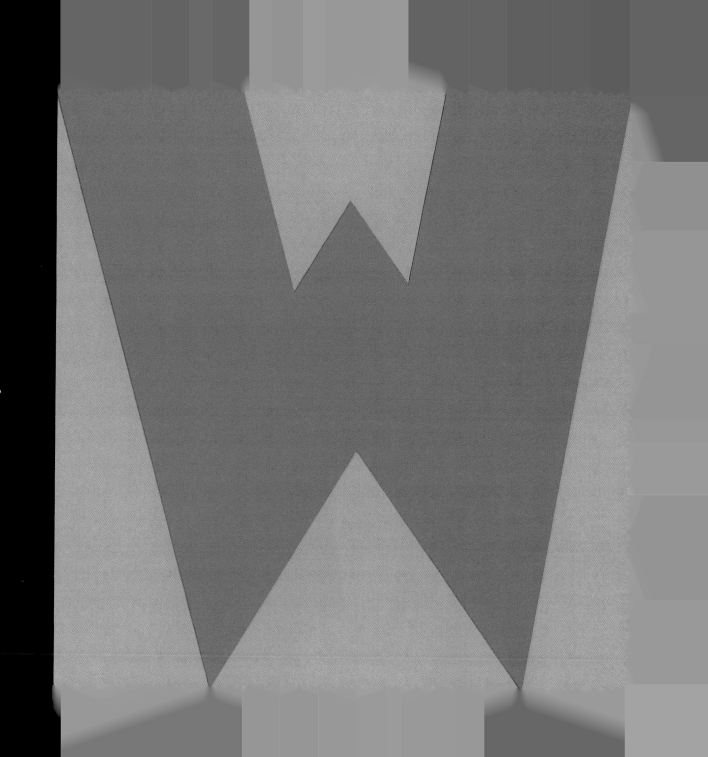

a mountain stream.

a treasure map's end,

a railroad-crossing sign,

a ballerina's shoe ribbons.

X imagines itself

a mermaid's tail,

Y becomes

a garden snake's open mouth.

a bend in the yellow brick road.

Z masquerades as

jack-o'-lantern teeth up close,

AUTHOR'S NOTE

When I was a child I loved lying in the grass on summer days and watching the clouds overhead. Above me floated rabbits, dragons, and dinosaurs, conjured by my imagination.

The powers of imagination and perspective fascinate me. They shape how we see the world around us. Many artists create art to be viewed from various angles, as well as optical illusions that toy with what is real and what we *think* is real.

For this book I chose the alphabet as a base, and began looking at the letters from different angles. I discovered it was a fabulous game, a kind of alphabet improv with many twists and turns along the way. Some letters immediately had a huge list of options, and other letters took more staring and squinting. Those were my favorites. I dragged family and friends in on the game, carrying letters in my notebook. "What do you see here?" I would ask. "How about this?" I was constantly delighted by the diversity of answers. Of course we will all see different things.

I hope that these pages of turning letters open up a conversation about looking at the world in other ways and that the readers will discover their own images in this familiar but always surprising world.